though
Activities

English for Short Courses

Bernard Seal

Longman

This book was developed by the author for the English Language Centre, Hove, where it was taught on two-week and three-week intensive courses. The helpful comments of teachers and students have been taken into account in the changes made for this edition.

Acknowledgements

Norma Williams, who typed out the manuscript of this book, was never anything but cheerful, patient and encouraging. Her importance in helping to get this book produced cannot be over-estimated.

I would also like to acknowledge the help and encouragement of Dr Ian Dunlop, Irene Andrew and the many teachers of the English Language Centre, Hove, who offered constructive criticism, useful suggestions and who had to put up with my ranting in the staffroom for so long.

To Claire Woolford, John Neil, Philippa Andrew, Stefan Szczelkun, Janet Beneyto and Susie Stenning – many thanks, too.

B.D.S.

Longman Group Limited
London

Associated companies, branches and representatives throughout the world

© Longman Group Limited 1980

Designed and produced by SGS Education Ltd., 8 New Row, London WC2. Edited by Janet Beneyto. Illustrated by David Godfrey, John Plumb and Barrie Thorpe.

All rights reserved. No part of this publication may be reproduced, stored in a retrieval system, or transmitted in any form or by any means, electronic, mechanical, photocopying, recording, or otherwise, without the prior permission of the Copyright owner.

First published 1980

ISBN 0 582 51570 X

Printed in Great Britain by Spottiswoode Ballantyne Ltd., London and Colchester.

Contents

	page
My Class	5

UNIT ONE JOBS AND WORK 7

At the Employment Agency	7
A Day in the Life of . . .	10
What do you Like?	11
The Jobs Game	11
How often do you . . . ?	12
Getting There	13
Taking the Bus	13
Following Directions	14
People and their Jobs	15
Project on Transport	16
Grammar Review and Homework Activities	18

LANGUAGE SUMMARY OF UNIT ONE
Review of present simple tense used to express habitual actions, likes and dislikes; *would you?* – requesting; *may I?* – asking permission; telephone numbers, addresses, dates and times; *oh, really?* – sounding interested; *could you tell me the way to?* – asking directions.

UNIT TWO HOLIDAYS 22

Where have you been?	22
The Rain in Spain	23
Time for some Prepositions	24
When did you last . . . ?	25
Have you ever. . . ?	25
What was your Holiday like?	26
Why? Why? Why?	28
Why do we go on Holiday?	29
Booking into a Hotel	30
Shopping	31
What a Terrible Holiday!	32
Project on Food and Drink	34
Grammar Review and Homework Activities	36

LANGUAGE SUMMARY OF UNIT TWO
Review of past simple tense used to express completed actions – contrasted with *have you ever?*; prepositions used in time phrases; *what was it like?* – asking someone to evaluate or describe; *it's windy out* – describing the weather; *in order to* + infinitive – expressing purpose; countable and uncountable nouns; *I'd like* – ordering in shops, hotels etc.; *much* and *many*.

UNIT THREE HEALTH 40

Biography of a Doctor	40
A Study in Three Tenses	41
The Dobbs' Family	42
At the Doctor's Surgery	43
Champion of the World!	45
A Guessing Game	46
More or Less	47
General Knowledge Quiz	47
Giving Advice	48
Doctors	49
Dentists	50
Project on Signs and Abbreviations	51
Grammar Review and Homework Activities	52

LANGUAGE SUMMARY OF UNIT THREE
Review of the present perfect simple and continuous tenses used for events and states starting in the past and continuing up to the present; *I've got a ____ ache / a pain in my / my ____ hurts* – describing your health; *oh, dear!* – sounding sympathetic; formation of comparative and superlative adjectives; *should and shouldn't* – giving advice.

UNIT FOUR LOVE AND MARRIAGE 56

Married Life	56
A Successful Marriage	57
A Conversation	58
What a Coincidence!	60
Making a Date	61
Love at First Sight	62
Cinderella – Picture Story	63
Ask and Tell	64
Computer Dating	65
A Computer Dating Form	66
Project: A Puzzle	67
Grammar Review and Homework Activities	68

LANGUAGE SUMMARY OF UNIT FOUR
Review of the present continuous tense to express future meaning and the temporary present; the *going to* future; expressing opinions; disagreeing; *so do I/neither do I* – agreeing; *I'm sorry. I'm afraid I can't* – regretting and turning down an invitation; *will you? / would you like to?* – invitations; *he asked me to / told me to* – reporting a request or a command.

ACTIVITIES – Listening Exercises and Structure Drills 72

UNIT ONE	72
UNIT TWO	74
UNIT THREE	76
UNIT FOUR	79

My Class

Name	Country	Age	Job/Field of Study	Married/ Single	No. of Children	Main Interest

Question	Answer
What's your name?	My name is _____
Where do you come from? (country)	I come from _____
Where do you live? (town)	I live in _____
How old are you?	I'm _____
What do you do?	I'm a/an _____
Are you married?	_____
Have you any children?	_____
What are your interests?	My interests are _____

Unit One

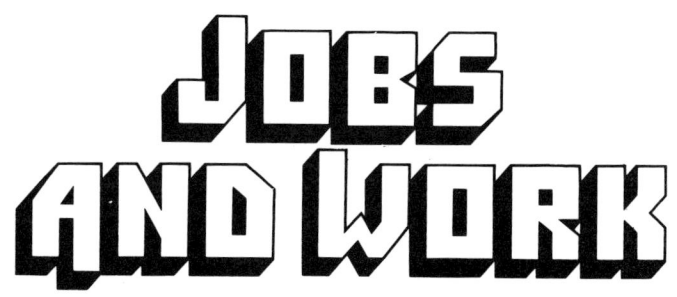

At the Employment Agency

ACTIVITY 1:
Practise this dialogue. Then YOU answer the clerk's questions. Imagine that you want to change your job.

Alice Saunders is a young and attractive girl. She is a hotel receptionist. She works in a very good hotel in London, but she wants to change her job because she doesn't like the new manager. Every day he asks her "Will you go out with me tonight?" Every day she says "No!" So now here she is in the employment agency looking for a new job.

CLERK: Good morning. Please take a seat.
ALICE: Thank you.
CLERK: Now then. What's your name?
ALICE: Alice Saunders.
CLERK: And what can we do for you?
ALICE: I want to change my job.
CLERK: Uh-huh. And what do you do at the moment?
ALICE: I'm a hotel receptionist.
CLERK: I see. OK. Well, let's write down a few details. What's your full name?
ALICE: Alice Mary Saunders.
CLERK: Could you spell your surname for me, please?
ALICE: S-A-U-N-D-E-R-S.
CLERK: And may I have your date of birth?
ALICE: 7th October 1959.
CLERK: Are you married or single?
ALICE: Single.
CLERK: And may I have your address?
ALICE: 9 Worthington Street, London, NW10.
CLERK: I'm sorry, could you repeat that?
ALICE: 9 Worthington Street, London, NW10.
CLERK: And your telephone number?
ALICE: 274 4011.
CLERK: Right. And . . . . . . what are you doing this evening?

ACTIVITY 2:
Go through these exercises.

Practice 1

    CLERK: **What do you do at the moment?**
    ALICE: **I'm a hotel receptionist.**

When we ask someone about their job, we say: "What do you do?"

Ask the person next to you: "What . . . . . . ?"
Answer: "I'm a/an . . . ."

Now ask the person next to you about the jobs of their husband/wife/brother/son/daughter/father/mother/next-door-neighbour, etc.

Question: What does your father do?
Answer: He's a/an . . . .

Practice 2

    CLERK: **Could you spell your surname for me, please?**

Now ask someone politely to:

1. close the door	3. open the window	5. explain this word
2. turn on the TV	4. answer the telephone	6. pass the sugar

Practice 3

    ALICE: **S-A-U-N-D-E-R-S**

Can you say the English alphabet?

**A B C D E F G H I J K L M
N O P Q R S T U V W X Y Z**

Practice 4

    CLERK: **May I have your date of birth?**

"May I . . ." is a polite way to ask permission to do something. For example, you are in a friend's car and you want to smoke, so you say "May I smoke in your car?"

• Now ask permission to:

1. use the telephone	3. have a bath	5. have a look at the newspaper
2. watch TV	4. borrow the car	6. listen to the radio

Note: You can also say: "*Can I* have your date of birth please?" "May I . . ." is more formal.

Practice 5

ALICE: **7th October...**

What's the date today, tomorrow, yesterday?
When is your birthday?

Do you know the names of all the months?

Note: There are two ways of *saying* the date in English:
1. The (1st, 2nd, 3rd) of (month)
   eg The first of June.
2. (Month) the (4th, 5th, 6th)
   eg June the first.

Practice 6

ALICE: **9, Worthington Street...**

What is YOUR address?

Note: In Britain we say the number of the house first, the name of the street second and then the town.

Practice 7

ALICE: **274 4011**

Say the following telephone numbers:

| 1. 889 4891 | 3. 01-455 3162 | 5. 0273-721771 |
| 2. 640598 | 4. 01-276 4039 | |

Note: When we say a telephone number, we say:
1. each number eg 721 = seven-two-one.
2. 0 as oh eg 903 = nine-oh-three.
3. double when two numbers are the same and together
   eg 55 = double five.

Practice 8

Fill out this job application form.

Full Name	Sex	Date of Birth
Permanent Address		Place of Birth
Name and Address of Current Employer		

A Day in the Life of...

ACTIVITY 3:
Look at these pictures and say what these people do.

He's a ...   He's a ...   She's a ...   She's a ...

He's a ...   She's a ...   He's a ...   She's an ...

What does a hairdresser do? Talk about his job.

| He | cuts
styles
washes | hair |

Now talk about the other jobs in the pictures.

Pair practice

Look at the pictures again. Choose one of these jobs and then ask and answer questions with the person sitting next to you.

    A: What do you do?
    B: I'm a ......
    A: Oh, really. Tell me about your day.
    B: Well, I ...... and I ....

When you are listening to your neighbour, try to sound interested by saying words like: "Yes .... Mm .... That's interesting .... Really .... Uh-huh .... Oh .... I see ...."

More pair practice

Now answer the same questions. This time talk about YOUR day.

What do you Like?

ACTIVITY 4:
Answer questions about what you like and don't like, using the short answer form.

    A: Do you like milk?
    B: Yes, I do./No I don't.

Pair practice
Ask the person sitting next to you what he or she likes.
Here are some ideas to help you:

Then answer questions about what other students in the class like and don't like. Answer like this:

    A: Does he/she like . . . ?
    B: Yes, he/she does./No he/she doesn't.

The Jobs Game

ACTIVITY 5:
Write the name of a job on a piece of paper. Don't show it to the class.

Now ask questions to find out the job on the piece of paper of each student. Only ask questions where the answer is "Yes" or "No". Start your questions with "Do you . . . ?"
Here are some questions to help you:

Do you work inside?   Do you wear a uniform?   Do you earn a lot of money?   Do you need special training?   Do you sell something?

How often do you...?

ACTIVITY 6:
Look at these phrases:

Every	night day week

once twice three times four times	a	day week month year

Now answer these questions:

How often do you...
wash your hair?
go shopping?
go out for dinner?
do any sport?
go to the cinema?
go to a football match?
go dancing?
buy a pair of shoes?
watch TV?
read the newspaper?

ACTIVITY 7:
Put these words into the scale from ALWAYS to NEVER:

*always*_____
_____
_____*never*

sometimes
often
rarely
usually
not often

ACTIVITY 8:
Look at the position of these words in the sentence:

I	often usually never	get up at 8.00.

Now answer these questions using the above word order:

When do you get up?
What do you do on Sundays?
What do you drink with your meals?
Where do you eat lunch?
When do you take your holidays?
What do you have for breakfast?
When do you go to bed?
Which newspapers do you read?

Pair practice
Now ask the person sitting next to you the above questions and think of *some more questions* of your own. Then report back to the class and tell them what he or she usually does.

He	sometimes usually often	gets up at 8.00.

Getting There

ACTIVITY 9:
Look at this short dialogue:

A: How do you get to work/school?
B: I usually go by bus.
A: Really? How long does it take?
B: Ooh! It usually takes about 15 minutes.

How do you get to work or to school? Do you go by bus, by train, by bike or do you walk?

Pair practice
Now practise the dialogue with the person sitting next to you and tell him/her how you get to work or to school and how long it takes.

Taking the Bus

ACTIVITY 10:
Listen to this dialogue:

Practice 1
Ask someone to tell you which bus goes to:

1. Churchill Square
2. The Town Hall
3. Nevill Road
4. The ABC Cinema
5. The Football Ground
6. Preston Street

Practice 2
A bus arrives at a bus stop in London. Ask someone if the bus goes to:

1. The Tower of London
2. Buckingham Palace
3. Trafalgar Square
4. Westminster Abbey
5. The Tate Gallery
6. Regent's Park

Following Directions

ACTIVITY 11:
When you are in a strange place you will find the following phrases very useful. Practise saying them.

| Excuse me. Can you tell me | the way to
how to get to | Oxford St?
Regent St?
Fleet St? |

Here are some of the things people will say when you ask them the way:

> Go up/Go down/Go along this street . . .
> Go back the way you were coming . . .
> Turn left/Turn right . . .
> Take the first turning on the left . . .
> Take the third turning on your right . . .
> At the next corner/At the traffic lights . . .
> Go past the . . .
> Go over the bridge . . .
> On the other side of the street . . .
> When you get to the . . . ask again.
> You can't miss it.

And here's a sentence for you if someone asks you the way:

> I'm sorry, I'm a stranger here myself.

Practice

 Now listen to these directions and try to follow them on the map.

People and their Jobs

ACTIVITY 12:
Read the following passages and answer the questions.

Lucy works in a travel agency. Her salary is very low. She only gets three weeks' holiday a year and she works long hours. But Lucy doesn't mind, because she enjoys her work. She has a nice boss and she meets a lot of people during the day. Her work is interesting and varied. Also, every year her company gives her a free two-week holiday in Europe.

> 1. Imagine you meet Lucy. Ask her questions about her job.
> 2. Think of other jobs with good 'perks'.
> 3. What are good working conditions?

Paul works on a car assembly line in a factory. He is a skilled worker and he does a lot of overtime; so at the end of each week he takes home quite a good wage. However, he doesn't enjoy his work. He finds it boring and monotonous. He gets four weeks' holiday a year, but because there are often strikes in the factory, he doesn't usually work 48 weeks a year.

> 1. Imagine you meet Paul. Ask him questions about his job.
> 2. Would you like to work in a factory? Why? Why not?
> 3. Are there a lot of strikes in your country?

Tom is unemployed. He is a university graduate and he has a degree in sociology. However, Tom cannot find a good job. Each week he receives a little money from the government called "Social Security". With this money he pays the rent and buys his food, but at the end of the week he is always "broke".

> 1. Imagine you meet Tom. Ask him questions about his life.
> 2. Does your government give money to the unemployed?
> 3. Are there many unemployed graduates in your country?

Mr Charles is a successful businessman. He is a company director. He earns a lot of money, and he also pays a lot of income tax. He is 64 and next year he is going to retire. He will get a good pension from his company and also an old age pension from the state. He is looking forward to his retirement. He wants to read a lot and go fishing.

1. Ask Mr Charles some questions.
2. What is the usual retirement age in your country?
3. Can you talk about pension schemes in your country?

Project on Transport

PART 1:

1. Name these parts of the car:

2. Name these parts too:

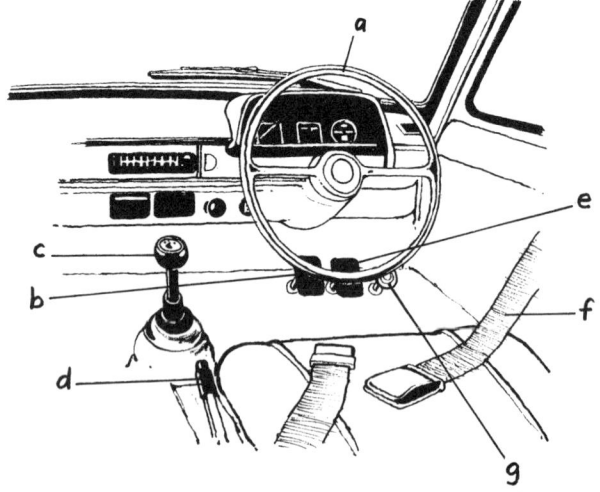

3. In Britain what is a car's fuel called?
   a) gas   b) petrol   c) oil   d) petroleum
4. How many litres are there in one gallon?
5. a) How much does one gallon cost in England?
   b) How much does one gallon cost in your country?

6. a) How many kilometres is 5 miles?
   b) How many miles is 160 kilometres?
7. What does m.p.h. mean?
8. Compare the speed limit on
   a) a motorway in England.
   b) a motorway in your country.
9. Look at this British car's number plate. What is the significance of the last letter?
10. Find out which city in England is the centre of the car industry.

ABC 132K

PART 2:

Complete these sentences with the words on the right:

1. We sailed across the Atlantic in a big _____.

2. We took the Channel _____ from Newhaven to Dieppe.

3. The postman came in a _____ and delivered the parcels.

4. Catch a number 16 _____ to Victoria and then go by _____ on the Victoria Line.

5. The _____ delivered the sand to the building site.

6. You must wear a crash helmet when riding a _____.

7. I flew to New York in a _____ with 400 other passengers.

8. It takes 35 minutes to go from Dover to Calais by _____.

9. You can now fly to New York in 3 hours 25 minutes if you go by _____.

10. The Americans launched another _____ yesterday from Cape Kennedy.

lorry
tube
Concorde
ferry
rocket
bus
motorbike
van
hovercraft
ship
Jumbo jet

Grammar Review and Homework Activities for Unit One

1. THE PRESENT SIMPLE TENSE

When we form the present simple tense, we use the base verb – unchanged. But when the subject of the sentence is third person singular, we add "s" and sometimes "es" to the base verb.

Base verb	Third person singular	Other subjects
spend	she spends	you spend
take	it takes	we take
watch	he watches	they watch

Formation of the negative

Negative statements in English need an auxiliary verb (or a modal verb) after which we put the word "not" or the short form "n't".
The present simple tense has no auxiliary verb and, therefore, we bring in the helping verb "do" as somewhere to place the word "not/n't". The auxiliary verb takes the tense and shows us the number and person of the subject. The base verb does not change.

Base verb	Third person sing. neg.	Other subjects
write	he doesn't write	they don't write
sing	she doesn't sing	you don't sing
watch	she doesn't watch	we don't watch

Formation of questions

Again we need the helping verb "do". This time it is needed because most questions in English are formed by changing the position of the subject and the auxiliary verb. There is no auxiliary verb in the present tense, so we use the present tense of the verb "do" and place that in front of the subject of the question.

Base verb	Third person singular	Other subjects
speak	Does he speak?	Do they speak?
play	Does she play?	Do you play?
touch	Does it touch?	Do we touch?

Uses of the present simple tense

We usually use the present tense when we talk about an *action* that we do regularly, every day, once a year, often, usually, sometimes, etc. We also use it to describe an emotional, intellectual or perceptual *state*.

Regular actions	States
John smokes 20 cigarettes a day.	I like this music.
Do you play chess?	He knows the answer.
The post usually arrives at 8.00.	Do you understand?
I watch the news on TV every night.	I hear a strange noise.

2. Write sentences containing true information. Use the present simple tense and the time expressions in brackets.

Example: **My mother makes breakfast every morning.** (every morning)

1. _____ (on Sundays)
2. _____ (sometimes)
3. _____ (every day)
4. _____ (once a month)
5. _____ (usually)
6. _____ (always)
7. _____ (twice a day)
8. _____ (every year)

3. Complete these sentences with a negative statement.

Example: He smokes a pipe, but he **doesn't smoke cigarettes.**

1. He drinks whisky, but he _____
2. I like music, but I _____
3. She understands the question, but she _____
4. He writes to his sister, but he _____
5. They speak German, but they _____
6. I often play cards, but I _____

4. Imagine you see this advertisement in the newspaper:

English person wants a penfriend from abroad. Please write with details.

Write a letter and tell him/her about yourself.
Write about the following:

– your age	– your house
– your interests	– your town
– your family	– what you look like
– your job/school	– what you do every day
– where you live	– why you want a penfriend

Your address
Date

Dear _____,

_____
_____
_____
_____
_____
_____

Yours Sincerely,

19

5. Read about Jim Brown. For each sentence think of a question which will give you the missing information and write them below. The correct question word is given to you.

Jim Brown lives in _____ (1). Every morning he gets up at _____ (2).

He takes a shower and then he wakes _____ (3).

For breakfast he usually eats _____ (4).

Then he leaves his house at _____ (5). He works in _____ (6).

He goes to work by _____ (7). It takes him _____ (8) to get there.

He likes his work, because _____ (9).

But he doesn't earn very much – only _____ (10) a year.

1. Where *does he live?* _____
2. When _____
3. Who _____
4. What _____
5. When _____
6. Where _____
7. How _____
8. How long _____
9. Why _____
10. How much _____

Now here is the missing information. Put it into the paragraph in the appropriate spaces.

---

he meets a lot of people   his wife and children
£3,000   25 minutes   bus   bacon and eggs
7.00   a department store   Dover   8.30

6. You are going to give a party. Look at the map on page 12. You live near the park. Your friends will arrive at the railway station. Write the directions on the invitation.

> Come to a party at 8pm on Saturday Nov. 20th at 5 Park View, Nottingham. Directions from the station –

7. Vocabulary from Unit One

a) Complete this with other months.

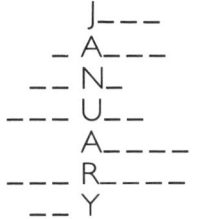

b) Complete this with the other days

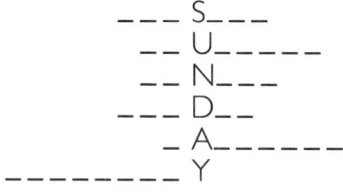

c) Fill in the spaces with suitable words from Unit One.

1. "How much do you _____ a week?" "About £100."

2. "How long does it _____ you to get here?" "20 minutes."

3. My grandfather gets a _____ from the state. It's £20 a month.

4. She's a _____. She looks after sick people.

5. "What do you do? "Nothing. You see I'm _____. I can't find a job."

6. "What is your date of _____?" "17th August 1958."

7. I don't like my job. It's very _____.

8. "Why is the factory empty?" "The workers are on _____."

9. My _____ is £400 a month.

10. "How _____ do you go swimming?" "Twice a week."

11. "Can you tell me the _____ to Robert Street?"

12. "Your first name is Mike. What is your _____?" "Whiteside."

Unit Two

Where have you been?

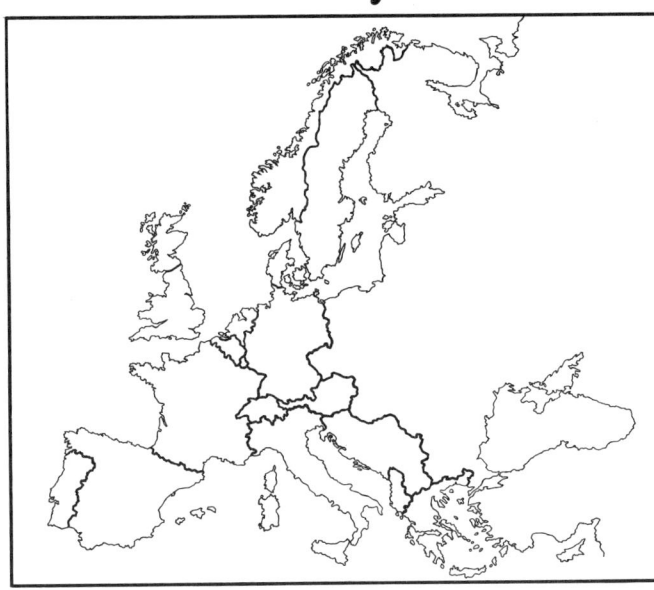

France
Spain
Germany
Denmark
Norway
Italy
Greece
Yugoslavia
Portugal
Switzerland
Scotland
Austria
Sweden
Holland

ACTIVITY 13:
Answer questions about which countries you have been to, using the short answer form:

Now look at the following dialogue. Notice the tense change when we are talking about a particular completed action in the past.

Pair practice
Now ask the person sitting next to you if they have been to the countries on the map. If they answer "Yes," ask them when they were there and for how long.

The Rain in Spain

ACTIVITY 14:
Answer the following questions and then read the passage:

1. Do you get a suntan or sunburn, when you sunbathe?
2. Do you ever get depressed? What do you do? Laugh? Cry? Eat? Sleep?
3. What is a heatwave? Describe really hot weather in your country.

Three years ago Robert Merryweather went to Majorca for his holiday. He spent two weeks sunbathing on the beach and got a beautiful tan. Last year, in August, he went there again. On the third day he was there it started to rain. It rained for ten days. Then at two o'clock in the afternoon, while Robert was in the airport waiting for his flight back to England, the sun came out at last. Feeling very depressed, he went to the newspaper stand and bought an English newspaper. The headlines read:

HEATWAVE IN ENGLAND COMES TO AN END

The following sentences are false. Can you say why?
1. Robert Merryweather was in Spain in the spring.
2. He went to Spain by train.
3. He stayed in Spain for a month.
4. His return flight left in the morning.
5. While he was in Spain, the weather in England was bad.
6. It rained every day he was there.

Now write the correct sentences here:

1. _____
2. _____
3. _____
4. _____
5. _____
6. _____

Time for some Prepositions

ACTIVITY 15:
Prepositions cause many problems for learners of English. You must learn which prepositions follow certain words and which are used in certain idioms and phrases.

Here is a list of prepositions which are used in TIME expressions

At	a precise point of time – at midnight, at 4.30.
In	a part of the day – in the morning, in the evening.
On	a date – on November 8th, on July 20th.
On	a day of the week – on Monday(s), on Friday(s).
On	a day of the week and part of that day – on Sunday morning.
In	a month – in May, in September, in January.
In	a season – in (the) winter, in (the) summer.
In	a year – in 1977, in 400 B.C.
At	religious festivals – at Christmas, at Easter.
For	a length of time – for two days, for six weeks.
Ago	the length of time from now to the past – 2 days ago. (Use with the past tense only.)

Now complete the following sentences with an expression of TIME:

1. I was born in _____.

2. My birthday is in _____.

3. My birthday is on _____.

4. I was born _____ ago.

5. I was born at _____ in the _____.

6. I was born on a _____.

And complete these sentences with a PREPOSITION:

7. __ August, ____ the last Monday of the month, there is a national holiday in Britain.

8. Most shops open ___ 9 o'clock ___ the morning and close ⁰___ 5.30.

9. English people send cards to their friends _____ Christmas.

10. There was a great fire in London _____ 1666.

11. ____ November 5th many people have firework parties.

12. People are happier ___ Friday afternoons than ___ Monday mornings.

When did you last...?

ACTIVITY 16:
Look at these expressions of PAST TIME. Use expressions like these to help you do the exercise.

yesterday	2 days ago	on + day
last week	3 weeks ago	in + month
last month	4 months ago	in + year
last year	5 years ago	

Say when you last did the following:

had a holiday	travelled by train
went to the cinema	took an examination
flew in an aeroplane	went dancing
ate fish	made a telephone call
wrote a letter	bought some new clothes

Pair practice

Ask these questions to the person sitting next to you. Begin each question like this:

"When *did* you last (VERB).......?"

Have you ever....?

ACTIVITY 17:
Find out about the experiences of people in your class by asking general questions about their past.

"Have you ever.......?"

If the answer is, "Yes, I have" then ask more questions and get the details. This time the questions are in the past tense:

"Where did you.......?"
"How long ago did you.......?"
"Why did you.......?"

Here are some questions you can ask:

Have you ever

won any money?	met a very famous person?
been in a play?	been on a skiing holiday?
fainted?	written a letter to a
had a serious illness?	newspaper?
broken an arm or	lost anything expensive?
a leg?	experienced an earthquake?

What was your Holiday like?

ACTIVITY 18:
Practise this dialogue and then YOU answer the friend's questions. Talk about your last holiday.

Robert Merryweather had a very bad holiday in Spain, but his friend Sandra Castle went to Italy and had a wonderful time. Here she is talking to her friend in the street.

FRIEND: Hello. You look well. Where have you been?
SANDRA: I've just come back from Italy.
FRIEND: Oh. Did you have a good time?
SANDRA: Yes. Wonderful.
FRIEND: Where did you go exactly?
SANDRA: Rimini.
FRIEND: Did you go on a package holiday?
SANDRA: Yes, I did. It was very cheap.
FRIEND: Did you stay in a hotel?
SANDRA: Yes I did.
FRIEND: And how long where you there?
SANDRA: A fortnight.
FRIEND: Did you go alone?
SANDRA: No, I went with my boyfriend.
FRIEND: And what was the weather like?
SANDRA: It was fantastic. It was really hot every day.
FRIEND: What did you do most days?
SANDRA: We went swimming and lay on the beach.
FRIEND: And what did you do in the evenings?
SANDRA: Some nights we went to a bar or a disco and other nights we just stayed in the hotel.
FRIEND: Did you go on any excursions?
SANDRA: No, we didn't.
FRIEND: Oh. Look at the time. I must rush. See
SANDRA: you.
FRIEND: Bye.

ACTIVITY 19:

Go through the following exercises.

Practice 1

Find the words in the dialogue which mean:

very good	Did you enjoy yourself?
two weeks	special journeys to interesting places
a place to dance	a holiday organised by a travel company

Practice 2

FRIEND: You look well.
SANDRA: I've just come back from Italy.

Imagine you look pale, tired etc. and talk about what you have just done, or what has just happened.

You look	You look
pale	exhausted
tired	fed up
happy	angry
bored	miserable

Practice 3

FRIEND: What was the weather like?
SANDRA: It was fantastic.

Use this question form to ask the person sitting next to you about one of his/her holidays. Ask about the weather, the hotel, the room, the beach, the swimming pool, the bed, the food, the waiters. Here are some words ranging from good to bad to help you answer.

GOOD
fantastic
very nice
wonderful
very good

OK
not bad
quite good
all right
OK

BAD
not very good
terrible
awful
really bad

Pair practice

You can also answer questions by *describing*—giving a picture in words. Ask the person next to you about people in their families, about the town where they live, their homes, their cars, etc. Answer the questions with a brief description.

Practice 4

FRIEND: What was the weather like?
SANDRA: It was really hot every day.

In England people love to talk about the weather. Often strangers talk about the weather in bus queues or in shops. You don't only talk about today's weather, but also the weather yesterday and tomorrow. Here is a typical conversation:

How do you think this conversation continues?
   A: Hello. Lovely day today, isn't it?

When you come into a building, you can tell the people inside what the weather is like outside by saying:
   "It's......out."

Describe the weather outside if someone comes in and says the following:

1. It's chilly out.
2. It's freezing out.
3. It's nice out.
4. It's boiling out.
5. It's miserable out.
6. It's windy out.

Why? Why? Why?

ACTIVITY 20:

In English when we want to give a reason for an action we can use the expression: In order to + VERB. Usually we just use the preposition: to + VERB.

Only one of the following is correct. Which is it?

   I came to England a) for studying English
                    b) for to study English
                    c) to study English
                    d) for study English

Now give some reasons for the following:

   Why do people go to discos?
   Why do people go on diets?
   Why do people learn foreign languages?
   Why do people go to pubs?
   Why are you studying this book?
   Why do people go to libraries?

Why did the chicken cross the road?
To get to the other side.

Why do we go on Holiday?

ACTIVITY 21:
Look at these pictures and talk about why you go on holiday and why you think other people go on holiday. Under each picture write some reasons. Start each phrase with To + VERB.

Booking into a Hotel

Comparison of hotel prices:

Hotel	SINGLE				DOUBLE			
	B & B	+ Bath	Full Board	+ Bath	B & B	+ Bath	Full Board	+ Bath
The Royal	£14.25	£18.25	£26.95	£30.95	£26.50	£33.75	£49.25	£56.50
Atlantica	10.50	15.00	18.50	23.00	20.00	25.50	31.00	37.00
Kings	11.00	14.00	16.00	19.00	21.00	24.00	33.00	36.00
The Crescent	10.99	11.35	—	—	19.25	22.00	—	—
The Tatler	5.25	—	—	—	10.50	—	—	—

ACTIVITY 22:

Listen to this dialogue and then do the exercises.

RECEPTIONIST: **Good morning, sir. Can I help you?**
MR WILLIAMS: **Yes, I'd like a room, please.**
RECEPTIONIST: **Yes sir. What would you like? A double or a single room?**
MR WILLIAMS: **I'd like a single room with a private bathroom.**
RECEPTIONIST: **A single room with a private bathroom...let me see...room 503 is free...And how long would you like to stay?**
MR WILLIAMS: **Three nights.**
RECEPTIONIST: **Would you like full board, sir, half board or just bed and breakfast?**
MR WILLIAMS: **How much is full board?**
RECEPTIONIST: **Twenty pounds a night.**
MR WILLIAMS: **And bed and breakfast?**
RECEPTIONIST: **Bed and breakfast is fourteen pounds fifty.**
MR WILLIAMS: **I think, then, I'll just have bed and breakfast.**

Pair practice

Look at the hotel prices above and book into a hotel. Decide if you'd like a single or a double room, a bathroom, bed and breakfast, half board or full board. Notice that when we ask politely for something in a hotel, a shop or a restaurant we say: "I'd like..."

More practice

Look at the hotel's menu card and order a meal. Tell the waiter: "I'd like......"

Shopping

ACTIVITY 23:
Study this dialogue:

BUTCHER: Yes. Next. What would you like?
CUSTOMER: Have you got any minced meat?
BUTCHER: Yes, dear. How much would you like?
CUSTOMER: A pound and a half, please.
BUTCHER: Anything else?
CUSTOMER: Have you got any beef sausages?
BUTCHER: I've only got three left. How many did you want?
CUSTOMER: Three'll do. How much is that?

Notice when the customer asks for minced meat the butcher asks:
 "*How much* would you like?"

But when she asks for beef sausages the butcher asks:
 "*How many* would you like?"

We are now going to look at two types of nouns. Sometimes they are called uncountable and countable nouns, or mass and unit nouns. Here is a list of nouns. Can you put them into the two groups?

MASS	UNIT

water
book
machine
information
newspaper
question
oil
air
girl
plate
sand
sugar
telephone
rubbish

Pair practice
Now imagine you are in a shop that sells everything. Ask for various things so that the shopkeeper can reply in two different ways.

   A: Have you got any......?
   B: How much would you like?

   A: Have you got any......?
   B: How many would you like?

What a Terrible Holiday!

ACTIVITY 24:
Look at the following sentences and see if you can find a rule for when we use MUCH, MANY and A LOT OF in informal English.

He went to *a lot of* bars, but he didn't go to *many* interesting places.

He drank *a lot of* wine, but he didn't have *much* fun.

Now read this passage and do the following exercises. Robert Merryweather is talking about his holiday in Majorca.

**I have just come back from Majorca. What a terrible holiday! The weather was awful, the town was boring, the hotel was dreadful and I spent all my money.
It rained almost every day and there was a strong wind which blew from the sea, so that when it didn't rain it was impossible to sit on the beach.
When it's not raining in La Fea, that's the name of the town, there isn't much to do. There aren't many interesting places to visit. So I stayed in the hotel most days and read a lot of books and watched a lot of rain. In the evenings I went out to bars and discos and I drank a lot of wine. There are hundreds of bars in La Fea. The night life there is good, but I didn't talk to many people, because I didn't feel well.
The hotel looked beautiful in the travel brochure but when I got there I found it was small and dirty. Most of the meals were badly cooked and the waiters were slow and rather rude. I had a tiny room with one small window and a beautiful view of the local fish market. What a smell!
And what a noise! At five o'clock every morning the sound of lorries, fishermen and people at the market always woke me up.
I am back in England now and I need a holiday.**

Decide if the following sentences are true or false. If a sentence is false, write the correct sentence below it. Change the verb from negative to positive or positive to negative and make the necessary changes to the words:

   a lot of   much   many

Example: It didn't rain much.
         False. It rained a lot.

1. **He spent a lot of time on the beach.**

2. **He didn't spend much money.**

3. **He didn't have much good weather.**

4. **He didn't visit many places.**

5. **He didn't read many books.**

6. **There are a lot of bars in La Fea.**

7. **He didn't drink much wine.**

8. **He didn't speak to many people.**

9. **He ate a lot of good meals.**

10. **He got a lot of sleep.**

33

Project on Food and Drink

PART 1:

1. What are the names of the following and how do you cook with them?

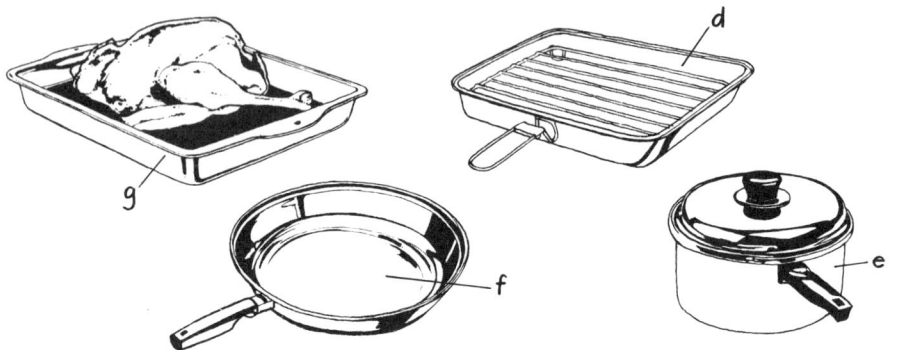
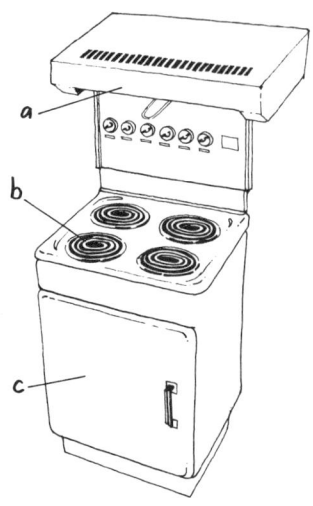

2. What does the abbreviation "lb" mean?
3. Write ½lb in words _____.

   Now write 1½lbs _____.
4. How many pounds make one kilo?
5. How many pints make one litre?
6. How much do the following cost in:

   (i) Britain   (ii) your country?

   a) a kilo of sugar _____

   b) a litre of cheap wine _____

   c) a pound of butter _____

7. A dozen eggs. How many eggs is that?
8. Fill in the spaces with the words on the right:

   a) a _____ of chocolates

   b) a _____ of bread

   c) a _____ of grapes

   d) a _____ of biscuits

   e) a _____ of sardines

   f) a _____ of cooking oil

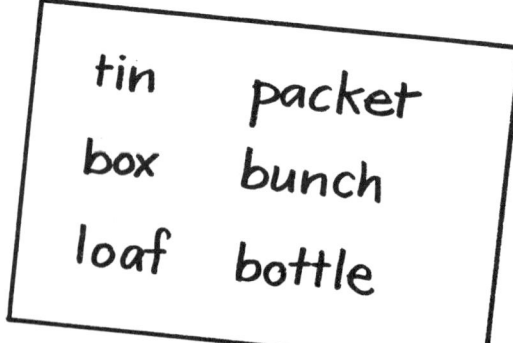

9. What is the "typical" English breakfast?
10. What is the difference between a chip and a crisp?

PART 2:
Which nationalities do you think go with the following foods? Here is a list of the nationalities. See if you can write them next to the food in the list below. Use each nationality only once.

> Italian French Spanish German Brazilian Chinese Swiss Indian Russian Scottish Japanese Irish Mexican Israeli Danish American Greek Swedish Portuguese Tunisian

1. _____ whisky
2. _____ rice
3. _____ hamburgers
4. _____ ice-cream
5. _____ sausage
6. _____ sardines
7. _____ oranges
8. _____ tomatoes
9. _____ stew
10. _____ bacon
11. _____ suki yaki
12. _____ wine
13. _____ chilli beans
14. _____ coffee
15. _____ caviar
16. _____ dates
17. _____ smorgasbord
18. _____ chocolate
19. _____ olives
20. _____ curry

Grammar Review and Homework Activities for Unit Two

1. THE PAST SIMPLE TENSE
Regular verbs
To form the regular past tense add the ending "–ed".
This ending has three different pronunciations.

Base verb	Past tense	Pronunciation of ending
watch	watched	/t/
live	lived	/d/
start	started	/id/

Irregular verbs
There are many irregular verbs in English. Fortunately we use the irregular verbs very often, and therefore it is not so difficult to remember them. Here are some examples:

go – went	come – came	think – thought
buy – bought	see – saw	write – wrote
do – did	make – made	take – took

Formation of the negative
Remember the negative in English is formed by placing the word "not" after the auxiliary verb. There is no auxiliary verb in the past simple tense, so we use "do" as a helping verb. The auxiliary verb (not the base verb) takes the tense. Here the tense is past so the auxiliary verb must be in the past tense – "did". The past tense, then, is: "did + not + base verb". We usually say "did not" as "didn't". Here are some examples:

I went – I didn't go	I washed – I didn't wash
he saw – he didn't see	they came – they didn't come
we tried – we didn't try	she left – she didn't leave

Formation of questions
Again we need the helping verb "do" in the past tense – "did". When we make questions in English, we have to change the position of the subject and the auxiliary verb. There is no auxiliary verb in the past simple tense, so we bring in "did", our helping verb. "Did" shows that we are using the past tense, so the main verb is in the "base form". To form the past tense question, then, we use:
    did + subject + base verb
Here are some examples:

Base verb	Past tense	Past tense question
see	I saw	(What) Did you see
go	he went	(Where) Did he go?
arrive	she arrived	(When) Did she arrive?

Uses of the past simple tense
When we tell a story or talk about something which happened in the past, we usually use the past simple tense. We use it to describe a completed event in the past. When we use the past tense we must know *when* the event happened – yesterday, last night, 2 years ago, etc.

2. Put the following sentences, which are in the past tense, into the negative. Change the time word from last Sunday to yesterday.

Example: I cleaned my car last Sunday. *I didn't clean my car yesterday.*

1. I spoke to him last Sunday. _____
2. We watched TV last Sunday. _____
3. He rang me last Sunday. _____
4. She came over for tea last Sunday. _____
5. We went for a walk on the seafront last Sunday. _____
6. They played tennis last Sunday. _____

3. Here are some answers to questions in a conversation. Look at each answer and see if you can give the question.

Example: Question: *What did you do last night?*
Answer: Last night? I went to the cinema.

1. Question: _____
   Answer: Two old James Bond films.

2. Question: _____
   Answer: Yes. I thought they were very good.

3. Question: _____
   Answer: I went with Judy.

4. Question: _____
   Answer: Afterwards we went and had dinner at "The Eating House".

5. Question: _____
   Answer: No, it wasn't that expensive.

6. Question: _____
   Answer: I had entrecote steak.

7. Question: _____
   Answer: Judy had the roast chicken.

4. Complete the story with these verbs, which are in the past tense. Use each verb only once.

> thought ran lost went held drank entered
> fell pulled saw rang stood ate woke
> led came heard started put became

Travelling through the dark forest on my horse I ___lost___ my way.

Suddenly I ___saw___ a small house in the distance. I ___led___ my horse up to the doorway.

I ___rang___ the bell. No one ___came___ to the door. So I ___went___ inside.

On the table there was some food and some wine. I was hungry and thirsty so I ___ate___ the food

and ___drank___ the wine. Then I ___heard___ a noise. A tall man ___entered___ the room.

In his hand he ___held___ a gun. I ___became___ very frightened. I ___started___ to run.

I ___ran___ through the house and out of the door. Just outside, however, I ___fell___ over a cat.

Then it was too late. The man ___stood___ over me. He ___put___ the gun against my head and

___pulled___ the trigger. I ___thought___ I was going to die, but instead I ___woke___

up with a terrible headache.

5. Write a paragraph about a holiday that you have had. You can write about your journey, where you stayed, what you did, the weather, what you bought or about one interesting day in the holiday.

Here is an example paragraph:

> **Three years ago I went with some friends on a skiing holiday in the Italian Alps. We flew to Milan airport from London and then took a coach to Trivera. There was a lot of snow on the mountains and the sun shone every day. The snow conditions were great. We skied a lot and on some days I took lessons in ski school to learn new techniques. In the evenings we went to the local discotheque. We danced and drank and met a lot of people. At the beginning of the holiday I was an intermediate skier, but now, after those ten days, I am an advanced skier.**

6. We usually use "much" + uncountable nouns and "many" + countable nouns when the context is a question or a negative statement. In all other cases we can use "a lot of" + any noun. Complete this dialogue with "much", "many" and "a lot of".

Example: A: Is there _much_ to do in this town?

1. B: Oh, yes. There are _____ things you can do.

2. A: But, I haven't got _____ money on me tonight.

3. B: That doesn't matter. There are _____ cheap discos. We'll go to one.

4. A: Will there be _____ people there?

5. B: Oh yes. But not _____ people we know.

6. A: Well, let's go anyway. It's already 11. We haven't _____ time.

7. B: I can't come I'm afraid. My teacher's given me _____ homework.

8. A: _____ students never do their homework. Come to the disco.

9. B: Also, I haven't got _____ petrol in my car.

10. A: We'll go by taxi. Come on. It'll be _____ fun.

7. Vocabulary from Unit Two

a) Complete this with other European countries.

b) Fill in the spaces with suitable words from Unit Two.

```
- - - E - -
- - - N - -
    G - - - - -
- - - L -
- - - - - A -
- - - N - -
- - - D - -
```

1. "What's the weather _____?" "It's very windy."

2. It's very hot today. I want to _____ and get brown.

3. "She's from France." "Yes, I thought she was _____."

4. "Hello, Globe theatre? I'd like to _____ two tickets for tomorrow."

5. I need a key _____ open this door.

6. "Would you like full _____?" "No, only bed and breakfast."

7. I go _____ holiday every summer.

8. A person who wants service in a shop is called a _____.

9. She _____ the examination last week. Unfortunately, she failed.

10. "What would you like for your first _____?" "Soup, please."

Unit Three

Biography of a Doctor

ACTIVITY 25:
Read the following passage and then answer the questions.

David Winter was born and brought up in a small town outside Manchester. When he was very young, he wanted to become a fireman; but as he grew older he decided to become a doctor. At the age of eighteen he left school and went to Liverpool Medical School, where he studied medicine for six years. Then he left Liverpool and went to work in Newcastle as a junior hospital doctor for a year. They say most doctors marry nurses and in Newcastle, Dr Winter met and married Nurse Powers. The following year he and his wife moved to a small country practice in Wales. They stayed there for four years, but Dr Winter began to miss city life. So he managed to get a practice in London, where he's been working as a GP ever since. He doesn't like London very much; he thinks it's too big and unfriendly. In fact he's now looking for a job in Liverpool, which he left ten years ago.

1. In what year was was Dr Winter born?
2. Now complete this chart:

Town	Manchester	Liverpool	Newcastle	Wales	London
No. of years:					
From–To:					–NOW

3. How long did Dr Winter work in Newcastle?
4. How long has he been working in London?
5. How long did he live in Wales?
6. How long has he been living in London?
7. How long was he a medical student?
8. How long has he been a doctor?
9. When did he get married?
10. How long has he been married?

A Study in Three Tenses

ACTIVITY 26:
Complete these sentences with true information.

I lived in _____ for _____ years.

Now, I live in _____.

I've been living in _____ for _____ years.

I worked for _____ for _____ years.

Now, I work for _____.

I've been working there since _____.

Or if you are still at school:

I went to _____ School for _____ years.

Now, I go to _____ School.

I've been going to _____ School since _____.

Pair practice

Ask the person next to you where he/she lives and how long he's/she's been living there; where he/she lived before and for how long. Also find out where he/she works and how long he's/she's been working there; where he/she worked before and for how long.
If he's/she's a student, find out where he/she goes to school now and how long he's/she's been going there; where he/she went to school before and for how long.
Before you ask the questions, write them down here:

(live)   Where _____ now?

               How long _____ there?

               Where _____ before?

               How long _____ there?

(work/   Where _____ now?
go to
school)   How long _____ there?

               Where _____ before?

               How long _____ there?

When you have the information, report back to the rest of the class.

The Dobbs' Family

ACTIVITY 27:
Here are some facts about a problem family.

Name	At the moment	has been ... since
Mrs Dobbs	Has a job in a launderette.	last Monday
Mr Dobbs	Is in prison.	1974
Jane Dobbs	17 years old. Is living with a lorry driver.	May
Michael Dobbs	Married, living in Canada.	Last year
Jimmy Dobbs	12 years old. Is in hospital. Has pneumonia.	Friday
Grandma and Grandpa Dobbs	Are in an Old People's Home.	1978
Uncle Tom	Unemployed.	last December

Role play

Imagine that you are an old friend of Mrs Dobbs, but you haven't seen her for many years. Ask her questions about the family. For each member ask "How is she/he?" "What's she/he doing now?" and "How long has she/he been ... ?". Begin like this:

OLD FRIEND: Hello, Gladys. I haven't seen you for ages. How are you?
GLADYS DOBBS: Oh, I'm all right. How are you?
OLD FRIEND: What are you doing these days?
GLADYS DOBBS: I'm working in a launderette.
OLD FRIEND: Really? How long have you been working there?
GLADYS DOBBS: I've been working there since Monday.
OLD FRIEND: And what about your husband? How is he?
GLADYS DOBBS: ......

At the Doctor's Surgery

ACTIVITY 28:
Practise this dialogue. Then YOU answer the doctor's questions. Imagine you have a medical problem.

Mr Pale hasn't been feeling very well lately. He has just waited forty-five minutes to see the doctor and now he is with the doctor in his surgery.

DOCTOR: Good evening. Sit down. Yes? What's wrong?
MR PALE: Doctor, I haven't been feeling well for the last few weeks.
DOCTOR: And what exactly is the matter?
MR PALE: Well, I've got a slight headache.
DOCTOR: Anything else?
MR PALE: In the mornings I sometimes have a pain in my chest.
DOCTOR: Uh-huh. Any other problems?
MR PALE: Sometimes my back hurts.
DOCTOR: I see. OK. Well, I'm just going to examine you ... open your mouth ... say "ah".
MR PALE: Ah!
DOCTOR: Right. Have you been worrying much recently?
MR PALE: Perhaps a little bit, yes.
DOCTOR: Mmm. Have you been sleeping all right?
MR PALE: No, actually doctor, I haven't.
DOCTOR: What about your appetite? Have you been eating properly?
MR PALE: Yes, I think so.
DOCTOR: So you haven't lost any weight recently?
MR PALE: No, I don't think so.
DOCTOR: What do you do?
MR PALE: I'm a teacher.
DOCTOR: And are you happy in your work?
MR PALE: Well, not really, doctor.
DOCTOR: Look. Here's a prescription.
MR PALE: Thank you.
DOCTOR: Take one of these before you go to bed each night. Try to stop worrying and come and see me in two weeks.
MR PALE: Thank you, doctor. Goodbye.
DOCTOR: Goodbye.

ACTIVITY 29:
Go through these exercises.

Practice 1

    DOCTOR: And what exactly is the matter?
    MR PALE: Well, I've got a slight headache.

There are five "aches". They are:

Note: headache takes the indefinite article "a"

```
HEADache
BACKache
TOOTHache
EARache
STOMACHache
```

Practice 2

    MR PALE: I... have a pain in my chest.

This is another way of referring to a medical problem. It can be used for all parts of the body. "I have a slight/terrible pain in my..."

```
Feet stomach arm
shoulder finger
chest knee leg
```

Practice 3

    MR PALE: Sometimes my back hurts.

This is the third way of talking about a medical problem. It, too, can be used for all parts of the body. Say that these parts of the body hurt:

```
ankle eyes feet
little finger
neck toes chin
shoulder
```

Practice 4

Here are four more symptoms of illness:

```
a sore throat
a cough
a cold
a temperature
```

Pair practice

You have 'flu. Explain to a friend how you feel. Look at practice exercises 1, 2, 3 and 4 to help you with the expressions you will need. Your friend can express sympathy by saying things like:

Finally say:
    "Well, I hope you feel better soon."

Champion of the World!

ACTIVITY 30:
Read the following passage:

On June 24th 1964, Cassius Clay, alias Mohammed Ali, became heavyweight champion of the world. He defeated Sonny Liston in the sixth round of the fight, lifted his arms in the air and shouted at reporters, "I am the greatest!".

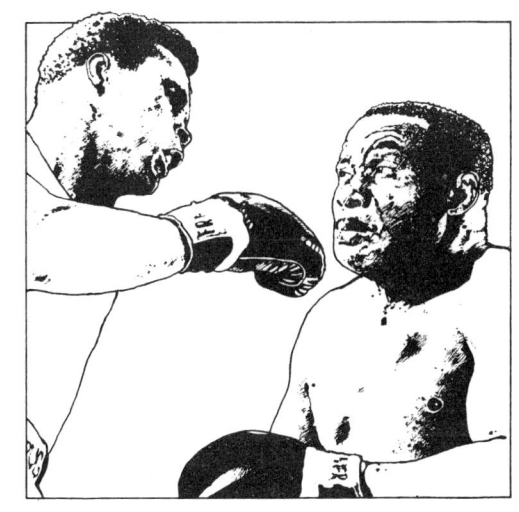

Make sentences comparing the two boxers.

	AGE	HEIGHT	BICEPS	REACH	CHEST	WAIST	THIGH	WEIGHT
CLAY	22	6'3"	52 cms	2.0 m	1.14 m	96 cms	63 cms	97 kg
LISTON	32	6'1"	54 cms	2.1 m	1.18 m	94 cms	62 cms	96 kg

Complete the following sentences comparing the two boxers. Use the words in brackets and make changes to the adjectives, if necessary.

1. Liston was ____*older than*____ Clay. (old / young / than)

2. _____ had a longer reach than _____ . (Liston / Clay)

3. Clay's chest was _____ _____ Liston's. (broad / small / than)

4. _____ was heavier than _____ . (Liston / Clay)

5. Liston was _____ _____ Clay. (tall / short / than)

6. Liston's waist was _____ than Clay's. (narrower / bigger)

Can you write the above sentences again? This time change the order of the names. If in the sentences above, Liston's name comes before Clay's, this time put Clay's name first. You will then have to change the adjective. Look at the example.

1. *Clay was younger than Liston.*

2. _____

3. _____

4. _____

5. _____

6. _____

A Guessing Game

ACTIVITY 31:
Look at the pictures of Mr and Mrs Wright and their niece and nephew, Barbara and Tim.
Choose one of the couples and then write down what you think their age, height and weight is.

	Age	Height	Weight
Mrs Wright			
Mr Wright			

	Age	Height	Weight
Tim			
Barbara			

Your partner will now try to guess the age, height and weight that you have written down, by asking questions like:

Is she/he	30 years old? 1m 60?

Keep giving your partner information in the following way until he/she gets the right answer:

No,	he's she's	(a little) (much)	younger / older than that. taller / shorter than that. lighter / heavier than that.

Now look at this ring.
How much do you think it costs?

Try to guess what your partner has written down by asking:

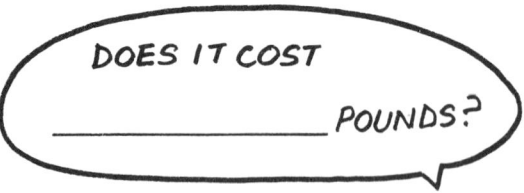

DOES IT COST _____ POUNDS?

It costs £_____

Answer your partner like this:

No it's	(a little) (much)	cheaper than that. more expensive than that.

More or Less

ACTIVITY 32:
In the following sentences, say what you think by using the words "more" or "less" with the adjectives.

Compare the following, using the adjectives in brackets.

1. Money	& health	(important)
2. English	& your language	(difficult)
3. Town people	& country people	(hospitable)
4. Trains	& planes	(comfortable)
5. Cats	& dogs	(independent)
6. Beer	& whisky	(alcoholic)
7. Japanese industry	& British Industry	(efficient)
8. English men/women	& men/women in your country	(attractive)
9. Playing a sport	& watching a sport	(enjoyable)
10. Cars	& motorcycles	(dangerous)
11. A package holiday	& a camping holiday	(expensive)

General Knowledge Quiz

ACTIVITY 33
Get into groups and discuss the answers to these questions. As a group, decide what the answers are. When you have answered the questions, think of some more of the same type to ask the other groups.

1. What is the longest river in the world? In Europe?
2. What is the largest land animal?
3. Where is the highest mountain in the world? In Europe?
4. Which country has the biggest population?
5. Which is the largest city in the world? In Europe?
6. Which is the fastest animal?
7. Which is the smallest bird in the world?
8. Which is the best selling book in the world?
9. Where does the oldest person in the world live?
10. Who was the most famous rock singer in the world?
11. Which is the second largest city in England?
12. Where is the highest waterfall in the world?

Giving Advice

ACTIVITY 34:
When we give advice we often use the words "should" and "shouldn't". It is not a strong command like "must". It tells the person that we think it is a good thing for them to do.

For example:
If we say this to a friend, it is a piece of friendly advice. Our friend can either follow the advice or ignore it.

Now read this story and give some advice.

Mr Muller is a German businessman. He has just had a heart attack and is now in hospital. Mr Muller is a heavy smoker and drinks heavily too. He works very, very hard, both at the office and at home. He also worries about his work. He drives a big, comfortable car, eats large business lunches and never takes any exercise. He is married with two lovely children, though he doesn't see them very often. The last time he had a real holiday was three years ago.

Mr Muller has survived his heart attack. Write five sentences:

> He should . . .
> He shouldn't . . .

_____
_____
_____
_____
_____

When we give advice to people, we often say "I *think* you should . . ." And when we want to advise people *not* to do something, we say "I *don't think* you should . . ."
Give advice to these people.

1. Someone who has a bad cold, a temperature and a sore throat.
2. Someone who wants to lose weight.
3. Someone who wants to learn to speak English very well. And someone who wants to learn your language.
4. A pregnant woman, expecting a baby next month.
5. Someone who is buying a new car. Suggest a make and model.
6. Someone who is visiting your country or town.

Doctors

ACTIVITY 35:
Study the vocabulary, read the passage and answer the questions.

Vocabulary

| TREATMENT |

– what the doctor does, his advice, the medicine you take. Also what you should do to get better.

| A SPECIALIST |

– a doctor who has expert knowledge of a particular problem, or of a special part of the body.

| AN OPERATION |

– when you are cut open by a doctor.

**There is a state medical service in Britain, called the National Health Service (NHS). Medical treatment provided by the NHS is free. It is free for foreigners, too.
Today many people think this service is inefficient. It is not difficult to see a GP (general practitioner), but they are often so busy that they can only spend a few minutes with each patient. If you want to see a specialist, you have to wait a long time for an appointment. If you need to go into hospital for an operation, you sometimes have to wait a long time – perhaps years!
People who can afford it, therefore, go to see private doctors. This is expensive, but the doctor can spend longer examining you and you don't have to wait long for an appointment.**

True/False questions
1. NHS patients pay nothing to see a doctor.
2. Foreigners have to pay a little to see a doctor.
3. You usually have to wait a long time to see a GP.
4. Medical treatment from a private doctor costs a lot of money.

Discussion questions
1. Do you pay to see the doctor in your country?
2. Do you have to wait long to see a specialist?
3. Talk about interesting personal experiences with doctors and hospitals.

Dentists

ACTIVITY 36:
Study the vocabulary, read the passage and answer the questions.

Vocabulary

> A FILLING

– when you have a hole in your tooth and the dentist fills it.

> AN INJECTION

– when the nurse or doctor puts a needle into your skin to put something into your blood system.

> AN X-RAY

– a photograph of part of the inside of your body.

In Britain, young people (under 21) and people on Social Security don't have to pay for dental treatment. Other people have to pay. But there is a maximum charge for treatment (in 1979 it was £7.00). This means if the dentist gives you one, two or three fillings, an injection, an X-ray and pulls out a tooth, you pay a little for each piece of treatment, but you don't have to pay more than the maximum charge. The government pays most of the cost of your treatment. There are also private dentists. People go to them if they want special treatment, like gold fillings or better quality false teeth. Some people go to private dentists because they don't have to wait for an appointment. It is almost impossible for foreigners in Britain to find a dentist who is willing to do work on their teeth on the National Health.

True/False questions
1. Everyone has to pay for dental treatment.
2. If one filling costs £3.00, three fillings cost £9.00.
3. You cannot get gold fillings from a NHS dentist.
4. Dentists don't like to give NHS treatment to foreigners.

Discussion questions
1. Why do people hate going to the dentist?
2. How could dentists make visits to them more enjoyable?
3. Do you pay a lot for dental treatment in your country?

Project on Signs and Abbreviations

PART 1: SIGNS

Where can you see these signs and what do they mean?

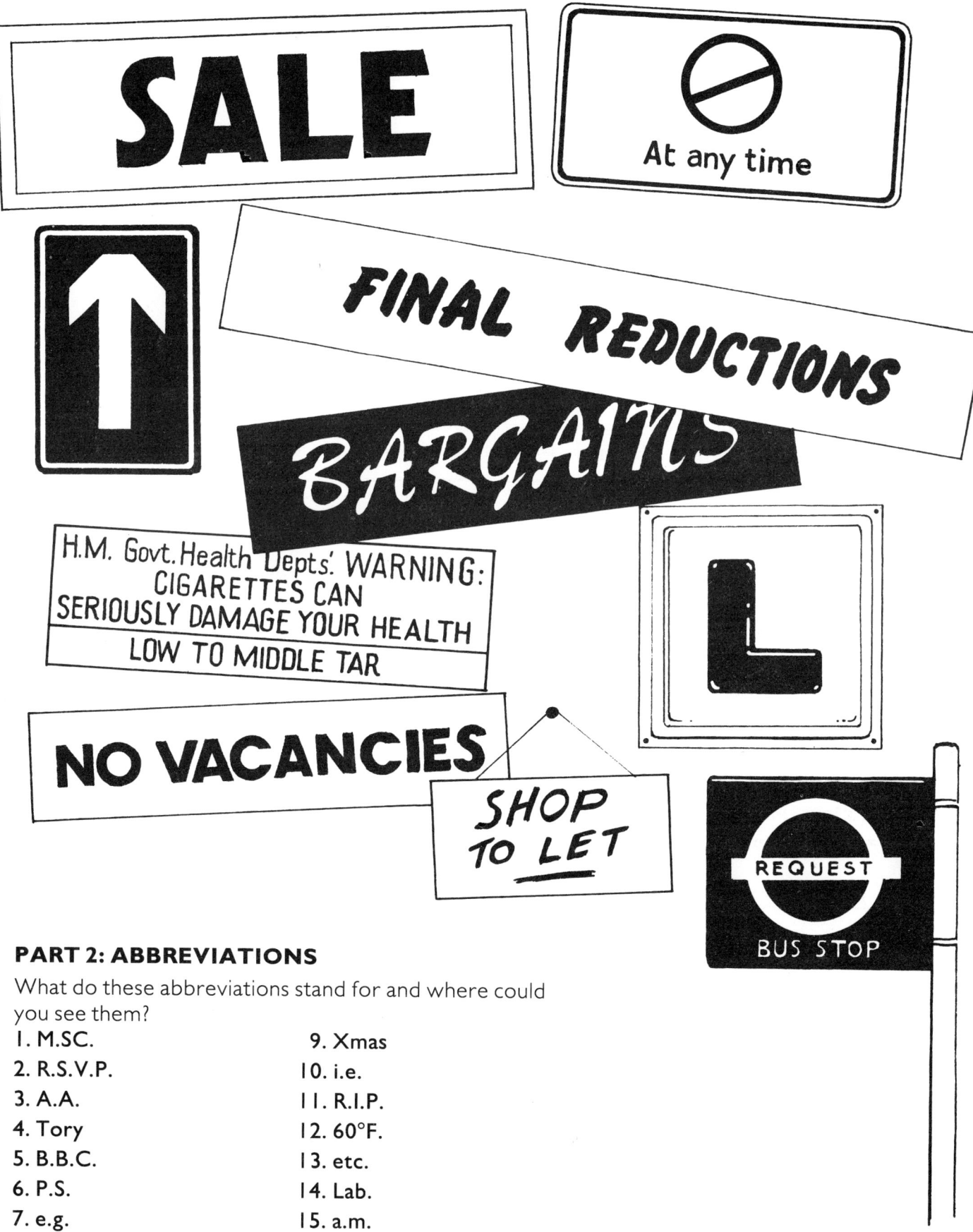

PART 2: ABBREVIATIONS

What do these abbreviations stand for and where could you see them?

1. M.SC.
2. R.S.V.P.
3. A.A.
4. Tory
5. B.B.C.
6. P.S.
7. e.g.
8. U.K.
9. Xmas
10. i.e.
11. R.I.P.
12. 60°F.
13. etc.
14. Lab.
15. a.m.

Grammar Review and Homework Activities for Unit Three

1. THE PRESENT PERFECT TENSE

Formation
The present perfect tense is formed by combining the present tense of the auxiliary verb "have" with the past participle of the main verb.
The past participle is the same as the past tense of regular verbs, but it is often different from the past tense of irregular verbs.
The negative is formed by adding "not" or "n't" to the auxiliary.
The question is formed by putting the auxiliary verb "have" before the subject of the sentence.

Base verb	Affirmative	Negative	Question
finish	I've finished	I haven't finished	Have you finished?
write	she has written	she hasn't written	Has she written?
leave	they have left	they haven't left	Have they left?

The uses of the present perfect
The best way to learn how the present perfect is used is to learn other words and expressions that we often use with this tense. Here are some of the uses of the present perfect tense, with words which often go with it, and some example sentences.

Use	Words used with	Examples
To talk about something which happened very near the present moment.	recently, lately, just, today	I have recently passed the exam. I have just won £1,000.
To talk about a state that began in the past and is still true in the present.	since + moment, for + period of time	They have been married for 3 years. She has had that car since 1975.
To talk about the past with some reference to the present.	already, not ...... yet, ever, never	Have you ever been to Italy? I have never eaten caviar.

It is often very difficult for learners to know when to use the present perfect and when to use the past tense. As a general rule, the past tense always describes an action or state in the past which finished at a definite point of time in the past. On the other hand, the present perfect in some way connects a past event to the present moment.

2. In this exercise decide if the past tense or the present perfect is correct. Then put the verb in brackets into that tense in the space.

    1. Recently she _____ (become) interested in medicine.

    2. Alexander Fleming _____ (discover) penicilin.

1. Recently she _____ (become) interested in medicine.

2. Alexander Fleming _____ (discover) penicillin.

3. Last weekend I _____ (catch) a cold and I _____ (be) in bed ever since.

4. My friend, Sam, _____ (never/have) flu.

5. First the nurse _____ (take) my temperature, then she _____ (take) my pulse.

6. The dentist _____ (give) me two fillings yesterday. But I _____ (not/yet/pay) him.

7. I _____ (not/smoke) today, but I _____ (smoke) four cigarettes yesterday.

8. Two years ago we _____ (get) married. We _____ (be) happy ever since.

9. "_____ you _____ (finish) your homework yet?"

   "Yes, of course, I _____ (do) it last night".

10. They _____ (be) married for ten years, and then he _____ (leave) her.

3. THE PRESENT PERFECT CONTINUOUS TENSE

Formation
In this tense there are two parts to the auxiliary verb: the present tense of the verb "have" + the past participle of "be" – "been". The main verb appears in the -ing form.

   have + been + VERB-ing

To form the negative the "not" or "n't" is attached to the first part of the auxiliary.
Example: She hasn't been sleeping well recently.

To form the question, the auxiliary "have" comes in front of the subject.
Example: Have you been sleeping well recently?
          What have you been doing?

Uses
The present perfect continuous is used like the present perfect, to show that an activity that started in the past:
   a) is still happening now,   or   b) has only just stopped.

4. People will often ask foreigners questions which begin: "How long" with the present perfect continuous. In this exercise, read the situation, think of a "how long" question and a possible answer.

Example: You are a foreigner living in England.

Someone asks you: *How long have you been living in England?*

You answer: *I've been living in England for 9 months.*

1. You are studying English.

Someone asks you: *How long* _____

You answer: _____

2. You are waiting for a friend. He arrives.

He asks you: *How long* _____

You answer: _____

3. Your teacher is teaching English.

You ask him: *How long* _____

He answers: _____

4. You are babysitting. The baby is crying. The parents come home.

They ask you: *How long* _____

You answer: _____

5. Rules for forming the comparative adjective

a) Adjectives of one syllable. Add "-er". Sometimes when the vowel is short and is followed by a single consonant, you must double the consonant.

b) Adjectives of two syllables, ending in "y". Change the "y" to "i" and add "-er".

c) Adjectives of two syllables. Usually "more" + adjective.

d) Adjectives of more than two syllables. Always "more" + adjective.

e) Irregular adjectives. There are only three.

a tall – taller
   big – bigger
   long – longer

b happy – happier
   busy – busier
   noisy – noisier

c distant – more distant
   tired – more tired

d beautiful – more beautiful
   comfortable – more comfortable

e good – better
   bad – worse
   far – farther

6. Give the comparative of the following adjectives.

lazy _____ late _____

dangerous _____ useful _____

fresh _____ interesting _____

exciting _____ early _____

fat _____ bad _____

7. Superlative adjectives
In forming the superlative the same rules apply as for the comparative.

8. Choose the correct answer a, b, or c.

1. John is the a) goodest b) better c) best footballer in the school.

2. Your bedroom is a) more dirty b) dirtiest c) dirtier than mine.

3. Yesterday was a) the more important b) the most important c) most important day in my life.

4. I'll buy the a) more cheaper b) most cheapest c) cheaper one.

5. a) The most frequent b) The frequentest c) The most frequentest word in English is "the".

> a. one syllable adjectives: add 'est'
> b. two syllable adjectives ending 'y': add 'iest'
> c. more than two syllables: 'most' + adjective
> d. irregular adjectives: best, worst, farthest.

9. Vocabulary from Unit Three
Fill in the spaces with a suitable word from Unit Three.

1. Bob is very hot. I think he has a _____.

2. "What's wrong?" "My eyes _____ and I've got a headache."

3. "Is he a specialist?" "No, he's a _____."

4. "Take this _____ to the chemists' shop and you can get the medicine".

5. Martha is _____. She's going to have a baby.

6. "Why are you holding your stomach?" "I've got a _____".

7. She's so fat. I can't put my arms around her _____.

8. The nurse brings food and medicine to her _____.

9. "How _____ are you?" "I'm one metre 75 cm".

55

Unit Four

Married Life

ACTIVITY 37:
Read the following passages and answer the questions.

This is Mr and Mrs John Cook. Today is their silver wedding anniversary. They have been married for twenty-five years. But it was twenty-seven years ago that John asked Miss Sarah Forrester to marry him. Sarah said "Yes." So John gave her a diamond engagement ring and they became engaged. They were engaged for two years. The wedding took place in church and Sarah wore white. After the wedding, they had a large party for their family and friends. At the end of the evening, they left the party in a Rolls Royce and went away on their honeymoon.

> 1. Do people become engaged in your country?
> 2. Do you give rings in your country?
> 3. Where is a popular honeymoon place in your country?

Roger and Mary have been married for three years; but they have been living together for five years. Roger is younger than Mary. He is twenty-five and she is twenty-nine. They decided to get married because they wanted to have children. They think that it is better for a child to have married parents. Now they have a six-month old daughter. Mary has an excellent job. She still goes out to work and Roger stays at home and looks after the baby. He also does the housework and the cooking.

> 1. What do you think is the best age to get married?
> 2. Children should have married parents. Discuss.
> 3. What do you think about Roger and Mary's marriage?

A Successful Marriage

ACTIVITY 38:
What do you think makes a successful marriage? Look at the following list and decide which you think is the most important, the second most important to the least important for a married couple to share.

Now get into groups and discuss the order of your lists. As a group put the list in order from 1 – 6. Compare the order you have in your group with the other group/s.

Here are some phrases to help you in your discussion:
 I would say that ......
 In my opinion ......
 If you ask me, I think ......

And some phrases to help you agree and disagree.
 I agree with you.
 I don't agree with you. I think ......

> same nationality
> same religion
> same class/money background
> same interests
> same educational background
> same age

ACTIVITY 39:
Now look at this next list and decide which qualities you think the ideal husband should have. Number the qualities from 1 – 10. Get into groups again and discuss your order. Say why you think some qualities are more important than others.

When you have discussed the ideal husband, put the qualities in order for the ideal wife and again discuss your order in groups.

Can you think of other qualities which the ideal husband or wife should have? Write them down. Then discuss why you think they are important with your group.

Here are some phrases to help you in your discussion:
 I think the most/least important quality is ......

 I think the ideal husband/wife should be ......

> good with children
> attractive to the opposite sex
> handy about the house
> a good sense of humour
> intelligent and well educated
> sociable
> tidy
> quite well off
> faithful
> hard-working

A Conversation

ACTIVITY 40:
Practise this dialogue. Then YOU answer the friend's questions.

 Alice meets an old boy friend in the street. They haven't seen each other for a long time.

FRIEND: Hello. How are you? I haven't seen you for ages.
ALICE: I'm fine. How are you?
FRIEND: Oh, I'm all right thanks. What are you doing these days?
ALICE: I'm still working in the hotel as a receptionist.
FRIEND: Really? And is that all right? Are you happy?
ALICE: Well, it's not too bad.
FRIEND: And what are your plans?
ALICE: I'm going to leave soon and get another job.
FRIEND: I see. Listen. I'd love to talk to you some more, but I'm afraid I'm in a bit of a hurry. What are you doing tonight?
ALICE: I'm afraid I'm busy tonight. I'm going out to the cinema with a friend.
FRIEND: Oh. Well ... what about this weekend? What are you doing on Sunday?
ALICE: No. This weekend is quite impossible. I'm flying to Amsterdam on Friday and I won't be back till Tuesday.
FRIEND: What a pity! Well, never mind. I'll give you a ring. What's your number?
ALICE: 274 4011.
FRIEND: And what's a good time to call you?
ALICE: I'm usually in most nights between five and seven.
FRIEND: Look. It's been really nice seeing you again. I hope we can get together soon.
ALICE: So do I. That would be nice.
FRIEND: Bye, then, I'll be in touch.
ALICE: OK. Bye.

ACTIVITY 41:
Go through these exercises.

Practice 1

FRIEND: What are you doing these days?
ALICE: I'm still working in the hotel....

In Unit One we looked at the question "Where do you live?" and the answer "I live in ......". Sometimes we use another present tense – the PRESENT CONTINUOUS. We can use this tense in questions when we expect a possible change or are asking about new circumstances in someone's life.

Complete these questions to an old friend whom you have not seen for a long time:

a) Where / you / live / now?
b) What / you / do / at the moment?
c) What / John / do / now?
d) Who / you / go out with / at the moment?
e) Who / you / work for / these days?

Practice 2

FRIEND: And what are your plans?
ALICE: I'm going to leave soon and get another job.

There are many different ways to express the future in English. The "going to" + verb future is used very often. We can use it when we feel "sure" that something is "going to" happen. Finish these sentences using "be going to + verb".

a) Look at those dark clouds. It _____ .

b) When my son grows up he _____ .

c) We _____ because we are in love.

d) Hurry up. The train _____ .

e) I _____ because it is the best car on the market.

Practice 3

FRIEND: What are you doing tonight?
ALICE: I'm going out to the cinema....

Here is another use of the present continuous. We often use this tense when we ask about someone's future plans. Practise asking these questions:

What are you doing	tonight? tomorrow? this weekend?	next Thursday? after school? on Monday?

We can also use this tense in the answer. Answer the above questions and say where you are going or what you are doing.

Practice 4

ALICE: **So do I.**

This short answer "So do I", shows that we agree with or do the same as the speaker. (**Note:** use with affirmative statements only.) Look at these sentences. If you agree with them say "Yes, so do I". If you don't think the same, say "Do you? I don't!"

I like tennis.	I think the English are friendly.	I come from Germany.
I like warm, sunny weather.	I usually sleep well.	I like cold beer.
	I live in a flat.	I want to get married soon.

What a Coincidence!

ACTIVITY 42

Read the following dialogue and practise the structures:
So + AUX + I – Neither + AUX + I.

Conversation in the Paris Metro

Pair practice:
Write sentences describing yourself:

what you can do	what you can't do
what you have done	what you haven't done
what you are going to do	what you aren't going to do
what you do or think	what you don't do or don't think
what you did last night	what you didn't do last night
what you are	what you aren't
what you should do	what you shouldn't do
what you have been doing	what you haven't been doing

Say these sentences to someone else in the class. They can then answer either:

So _____ I.   Really. I _____ n't.
Neither _____ I.   Really. I _____ .

Making a Date

ACTIVITY 43:
Have a look at Jane's diary.

SAT 20	Disco with Tom. meet 7.30	TUES 23	Badminton with Harry	FRI 26	FLIGHT A123 to Paris 8.45 pm
SUN 21	Cinema with Dick	WED 24	Dinner Party make Spaghetti	SAT 27	Day in Paris
MON 22	Stay home STUDY!!	THURS 25	Yoga class 6.30 bed early	SUN 28	FLIGHT A124 Arr. Gatwick 11.10 am

Now study this conversation between Jane and one of her admirers.

Guided Pair Practice

Complete this dialogue. Ask Jane out each night of the week.

JIM: Hello Jane. What are you doing on _____ ?

JANE: Oh, hello Jim. I'm afraid I'm busy on _____ .

I'm _____ .

JIM: Well, what about _____ ?

JANE: I'm sorry Jim, but I'm _____ .

JIM: Well, what are you doing on _____ etc.

Pair practice

Fill in four of the spaces below with an evening activity and then make a date with someone across the class. Find an evening when you are both free.

SAT	SUN	MON	TUES	WED	THURS	FRI	SAT

Love at First Sight

ACTIVITY 44:
Read the following story and then do the exercise.

The first time Michael saw Helen, he fell in love with her. It was love at first sight. The problem was how to win her love for him. First he tried to impress her. He asked her to fly to Cannes with him for the Film Festival. She refused. Then he asked her to come to Rome with him. But she said no. "Perhaps she likes the simple life," he thought. So he asked her to spend a weekend with him in the country. She refused that too. "Food. I'll try food," he thought and asked her to eat with him at Mason's, one of the best restaurants in London.

"No, thank you," she said and lowered her lovely blue eyes.

"She's so beautiful," he thought. "I will try one last question." And he asked her to marry him.

"Yes," she said. "I will. Mason's, Rome, Cannes, the country – what an exciting life we will have."

1. Write down all the things Michael asked Helen to do.

a) *He asked her to* _____

b) _____

d) _____

e) _____

2. Now write down what he said when he asked her to go to these places.

Cinderella

ACTIVITY 45:
Look at the following pictures and then tell the story. Try to use the structure: to tell someone (not) to do something.

Exercises
Make sentences.
1. What did the sisters tell Cinderella to do every day?
2. What did they tell her to do for them after the invitation had arrived?
3. Look at the last picture. What is going to happen next?

Role plays
1. Poor Cinderella wanted to go to the dance. Have the conversation between her and one of her sisters when they received the invitation.
2. Look at picture 4. Have the conversation between Cinderella and the fairy when the fairy asked her why she was so unhappy.
3. Have the conversation between the prince and Cinderella after he has found her and asked her why she ran away at the dance.

Ask and Tell

ACTIVITY 46:
Do the following exercise. Remember that we use "ask" to report a polite request, and "tell" to report a direction or a command.

In the following sentences change the direct speech to indirect speech, as in the examples. Decide from the situation if "ask" or "tell" is the correct reporting verb.

Example 1
　Speaker: hitch-hiker to lorry driver
　Direct speech: "Could you give me a lift."

He asked the lorry driver to give him a lift.

Example 2
　Speaker: bus conductor to woman in the street
　Direct speech: "Catch the number 9 bus."

She told her to catch the number nine bus.

Speaker	**Direct speech**
1. young man to young woman	"Will you marry me?"
2. General to soldier	"Kill the prisoner."
3. friend to friend	"Don't listen to her."
4. teacher to class	"Be quiet."
5. friend to friends	"Can you wait for me?"
6. student to student	"Would you like to dance?"
7. you to a stranger	"Could you help me, please?"
8. girl to ex-boy friend	"Don't phone me again."

Computer Dating

ACTIVITY 47:
Read the following passage and answer the questions.

If you are not married in Britain by the age of forty, people think that you are "odd". The average age that people get married in Britain is 22. There are, however, seven million unmarried people over 21. How do single people meet? Where do they go?

> a) Guess the meaning of the word "odd".
> b) What is the average of 7, 12, 16, 9, 11?
> c) Finish this sentence: "7 million people in Britain ......"
> *Discuss*
> Where do single people go to meet in your country?

There is one way single people, who are a little shy or lonely or who find it difficult to make new friends, can meet: through a computer dating service. Computer dating started in Britain in the mid-sixties at a time when computer technology was developing. Young people started to experiment with a new way of life. They had money to spend and exciting places to spend it.

> a) Guess the meaning of the words "shy" and "experiment".
> b) What does a computer dating service do for you?
> c) Computer dating started about: i) 1950 ii) 1960 iii) 1965
> *Discuss*
> What was the new way of life of the '60s?

Computer dating still continues today. All you have to do is fill in a form and describe yourself. You then send the form and twenty-five pounds to the service and they feed the information into the computer which then finds someone in its memory banks who is like you. Usually the computer will send you about six names and addresses and then you can contact these people and make a date.

> a) What are "memory banks"?
> b) Why do you have to "describe yourself" for the computer?
> c) Who finally contacts the date? i) You ii) The computer iii) The dating service
> *Discuss*
> What are the advantages and disadvantages of making dates through a computer dating service?

A Computer Dating Form

ACTIVITY 48:
Here is an example of a computer dating form. Complete the form and see who in the class is compatible with you.

Section 1

1. Age
- (3) 16 or under
- (5) 17–20
- (7) 21–25
- (8) 26–31
- (9) 32 and over

2. Class background
- (1) Working class
- (2) Middle class
- (3) Upper class

3. Education
- (7) University
- (5) Other Higher Education
- (3) A levels
- (2) O levels
- (1) No exams

4. Attractiveness
- (2) Unattractive
- (5) Quite attractive
- (7) Attractive

5. Cultural background
- (9) Northern & Central European
- (7) Mediterranean
- (6) Latin American
- (4) Middle Eastern
- (3) Oriental
- (1) African Negro
- (0) Asiatic

6. Religion
- (1) Protestant
- (2) Catholic
- (3) Jewish
- (4) Moslem
- (5) Buddhist
- (6) Hindu
- (7) Agnostic
- (8) Atheist

7. Politics
- (2) Left Wing
- (4) Centre
- (6) Not interested
- (8) Right Wing

8. Height
- (1) Tall
- (3) Medium
- (5) Short

9. Occupation
- (1) Unemployed
- (2) Student
- (3) Professional
- (4) Business
- (5) Office
- (6) Manual

Box 1
Fill in this box with the numbers which describe you from each list in order.

Section 2
Tick the things that you are interested in. Add up the numbers next to your ticks and put the total in the boxes.

Swimming	(2)	Television	(1)	Dancing/Discos	(4)
Tennis	(3)	Classical music	(4)	Going to parties	(2)
Sailing	(4)	Literature/Art	(3)	Pop music	(4)
Football	(2)	Current Affairs	(3)	Drinking out	(3)
Keep fit	(3)	Theatre	(2)	Eating out	(3)
Skiing	(4)	Science subjects	(4)	Cinema	(2)

Total =   Total =   Total =

Box 2
Put your three scores in this box.
e.g. (15, 6, 13).

Box 3
Add up the three totals and put them in this box. e.g. (34).

Section 3

Decide if you agree, do not agree or are unsure about the following statements. Put a circle around the letter in the columns representing your answer.

	Agree	Don't Agree	Unsure
1. Capitalism is preferable to Socialism.	A	B	C
2. Religion is important to me.	A	B	C
3. I prefer classical art to modern art.	A	B	C
4. I prefer classical music to pop music.	A	B	C
5. People get wiser as they get older.	A	B	C
6. Women with babies should not work.	A	B	C

Now count up the number of As, Bs, and Cs. Put the letter which occurs most in your answers in this box.

Box 4

Your four boxes are now as follows:

1. 2. 3. 4.

To find your ideal partner, look at the first four numbers in Box 1. These should be the same as your partners. All the numbers after this which are the same show even greater compatibility. The letter in Box 4 should be the same.

Project: A Puzzle

ACROSS

1. Costing a little (5).
4. 007, for example (3).
6. You can listen to this (5).
7. Thank you (colloquial) (2).
9. Not your (2).
10. Near the ground (3).
12. "____ I go?" (asking permission to leave) (3).
14. "Where is it?" "____" (4).
16. "Someone ____ ." (another person) (4).
18. "____' _ been raining since yesterday." (2,1).
20. Watched (3).
21. She works ____ a secretary (2).
22. An expression of surprise (2).
24. Help a student in class (5).
25. Not him (3).
26. Says what to do (5).

DOWN

1. Make hair short (3).
2. Soldiers (4).
3. Salary (3).
4. Like films before 1923 (6).
5. Not having much money (4).
8. In the morning (abbreviation) (2).
11. Opposite of dry (3).
13. You can ____ the phone, the door, and the question (6).
15. A positive answer (3).
17. "I'm sorry, I'm ____ ". (heard in class) (4).
18. "He's not, __ __ ?" (2,2).
19. Therefore (2).
21. Play a part on stage (3).
23. A student ____ to study hard! (3).

Grammar Review and Homework Activities for Unit Four

1. THE PRESENT CONTINUOUS TENSE

Formation
The present continuous tense is formed by putting the present tense of the auxiliary verb "to be" together with the "-ing" form of the main verb.

The negative is formed by adding "not" or "n't" to the auxiliary verb.

The question is formed by putting the auxiliary verb before the subject of the question.

Base verb	Affirmative	Negative	Question
work	He is working	He isn't working	Is he working?
listen	I am listening	I'm not listening	Are you listening?
run	They are running	They aren't running	Are they running?

The uses of the present continuous

a) We use the present continuous when an action that we are talking about is happening at the same time as we are talking.

Example: At this moment I am writing and my sister is making breakfast.

b) We can also use the present continuous with *future* meaning. In this case we must use a future time expression with the verb. It means that we have a plan to do something at a particular time in the future.

Examples: She's leaving tomorrow.
They are arriving on June 20th.

c) The present continuous can also be used to refer to the general present. In this case it is like the present simple. But we only use it like this to show that there has been a recent change.

Examples: I'm going out with Jean now. (Before, I went out with Mary.)
I'm walking to work these days. (Before, I took the bus.)

An important note on the present continuous
There are some verbs, when they have a particular meaning, which *cannot* be used with the continous form – the "-ing" ending. These verbs are called "state" verbs. They do not describe an active movement – an action. They describe a state which cannot easily change from moment to moment.

a) State verbs describe an emotional, intellectual or perceptual state:

like	know	hear
hate	think	see
want	understand	

b) State verbs also describe a relationship between things and people or describe the permanent state of something or someone.

own	have (possess)	cost
belong	resemble	weigh
contain	owe	

2. The present continuous and the present simple are often confused. In this exercise put the verb in brackets into the correct tense – simple or continuous.

1. Sometimes my husband _____ (bring) me breakfast in bed.

2. The family across the street _____ (own) two cars.

3. I think an insect _____ (climb) up my leg.

4. Mark has left Carol. He _____ (live) with Susan now.

5. Ask William. I'm sure he _____ (know) the answer.

6. You can turn the radio off. I _____ (not/listen) to it.

7. I can't afford butter any more. It _____ (cost) too much.

8. Look at Bernard. He _____ (jog). Do you know he _____ (run) four miles a day.

9. In our family we _____ (not/eat) meat. We are vegetarians.

10. It _____ (not/rain). Look! The sun _____ (shine).

3. Look at your watch. Write five sentences about people you know well. Say what you think they are doing at this moment.

Example: *(3.30pm) I think my mother is shopping at the moment.*

_____
_____
_____
_____

4. Imagine someone has just said something, which is true for you, too. Write down a statement to which you could give the answer on the right.

Example: *"I'm tired."* _____ "So am I."

1. _____ "So can I."

2. _____ "So have I."

3. _____ "So do I."

4. _____ "So am I."

5. _____ "So should I."

6. _____ "So did I."

5. What is "going to" happen? Look at the pictures and then write down what you think is "going to" happen next.

1. _____

2. _____

3. _____

4. _____

6. Read this telephone conversation. Bob is talking to Barbara.

What did Bob tell Barbara to do and what did he ask her to do? Write down the sentences below.

Ask _____

Tell _____

> RING MY MOTHER AND INVITE HER FOR THE WEEKEND. OH! AND WILL YOU TAKE MY TROUSERS TO THE CLEANERS? YES, AND DON'T FORGET TO PAY THE MILKMAN.... ORDER SOME CREAM FROM HIM, TOO. BY THE WAY, CAN YOU GET SOME MONEY FROM THE BANK?.... DRIVE CAREFULLY AND DON'T PARK THE CAR ON A DOUBLE YELLOW LINE. OH, ONE MORE THING, COULD YOU BUY ME SOME RAZOR BLADES WHILE YOU'RE OUT? THANKS. SEE YOU TONIGHT.

7. Read the story of Cinderella and then finish the story in your own words.

Once upon a time there lived a very beautiful girl. She had two ugly stepsisters, who were older than her. When the sisters saw that their younger sister was so pretty, they made her work hard in the house. She did all the housework and all the cooking. Most of the time she was covered in dirt, so that nobody could see that she was really very pretty. Her name was Cinderella.
One day when Cinderella was nineteen, a man came to the house with an invitation to a dance. The invitation was from the handsome prince who lived nearby. Everyone in the house was invited. But when the sisters saw the invitation, they said to Cinderella: "You can't go. The Prince doesn't want to see a dirty little girl like you, who has no nice clothes. Anyway, you must prepare our clothes and do our hair and look after the house while we're out."
So Cinderella did all the things her sisters told her to do. She washed, mended and ironed their clothes. She washed, brushed and styled their hair. She helped them dress and put on their make-up. And when they were ready to leave, they still looked ugly! The stepsisters left for the party and Cinderella stayed in the house, tired and unhappy. She had really wanted to go to the dance. She wanted to look nice, and to dance, and to see all the fine people. She sat down on a stool and started to cry. Suddenly there was a flash of light, and Cinderella looked up and saw a beautiful fairy in the room.
"Who are you?" asked Cinderella.
"I'm a fairy who has come to help you, Cinderella. Why are you crying?"
And Cinderella told her.
"Well, I can help you. If you really want to go to the dance, I can give you beautiful clothes and a fine carriage. But when it is midnight you must leave the dance. For when the clock has finished striking twelve, your carriage and your dress will disappear. And you will look as you look now."
"Yes, yes," said Cinderella, "I do want to go and I will leave before twelve o'clock." Then the little fairy clapped her hands. Cinderella looked at herself and saw she was wearing a beautiful dress. She rushed to the window and outside there stood a magnificent carriage with four white horses.

8. Vocabulary from Unit Four
Fill in the spaces with suitable words from Unit Four.

1. I feel very _____, I don't know anyone in this country.

2. "In my _____, you should find a new job."

3. "Is your husband _____?" "Oh, yes. He never even looks at another woman."

4. Yesterday was their _____ _____. They've been married ten years.

5. "Why don't you phone her up and _____ a date?"

6. "I don't _____ with you. You're wrong and I'm right."

7. After the wedding they went to Niagara Falls for their _____.

8. The _____ wife should be intelligent, attractive and fun.

9. "He told me _____ to worry."

10. "I think this is the end of the book." "So _____ I."

Unit One Listening Exercises and Structure Drills

Exercise 1

Write down the six words you hear spelt out on the tape.

1. The word is _____   2. The word is _____

3. The word is _____   4. The word is _____

5. The word is _____   6. The word is _____

Exercise 2

Say these dates, telephone numbers, years and times.

1.* 3.30	6.* 01-344 5218
2.* 30th August	7.* 12th February
3.* 772109	8.* 1.45
4.* 23rd April	9.* May 21st
5.* 9.05	10.* 22.40

Exercise 3

Look at these clocks and answer the questions about the Simon family.

1.  2.  3.  4.  5.

6.  7.  8.  9.  10.

Exercise 4

Listen to the examples.

Roger's a cashier.
That's interesting. Where does he work?

Mary and Susan are waitresses.
That's interesting. Where do they work?

Now you ask where these people work.

Exercise 5

Listen to someone talking about his friend's job. Ask questions to get more information. The question word is given below to help you. When you hear the answer, write it into the space below. Listen to the example.
   My friend works abroad.
   Where does he work?
   Saudi Arabia.

1. How much . . . ? _____

2. What kind of . . . ? _____

3. When . . . ? _____

4. When . . . ? _____

5. Why . . . ? _____

6. Who . . . ? _____

7. How often . . . ? _____

8. Which school . . . ? _____

Exercise 6

Listen to this photographic model, Tina, talking about a day in her life. Then answer the following questions.

1. Does Tina have a) a hot shower b) a cold shower c) both?

2. Which muscles does Tina exercise?

   a) _____ b) _____ c) _____

3. What are two foods she usually eats for breakfast?

   a) _____ b) _____

4. Does she finish her breakfast a) before ten b) about ten c) after ten?

5. How does she travel to work? _____

6. Does she usually eat lunch? _____

7. How many hours does Tina work a day? a) 4 b) 5 c) 6 d) 8 e) 11

8. What are two things Tina does when she gets home?

   a) _____ b) _____

9. Why does Tina often eat dinner in a restaurant?

_____

Unit Two Listening Exercises and Structure Drills

Exercise 1

Listen please.

He comes from England.
Really? He doesn't look English.

She comes from France.
Really? She doesn't look French.

Now continue in the same way.

Exercise 2

Look at these examples and listen, please.

(April)   When did they leave?
             They left in April.

(Monday)   When did they arrive?
             They arrived on Monday.

Now answer these questions, using the correct preposition, the past tense and the time phrases given below.

1. June	4. 6.00	7. 9.30
2. Saturday	5. Friday evening	8. the morning
3. 1949	6. 19th May	

Exercise 3

Listen please.

I booked some seats yesterday.
How many did you book?

I got some stamps yesterday.
How many did you get?

Now continue in the same way.

Exercise 4

Listen please.

Have you posted that letter?
Yes, I have. I posted it last night.

Have you been to the cinema this week?
Yes, I have. I went last night.

Exercise 5

Listen please.

Did you buy a lot of books?
No, I didn't buy many.

Did he lose a lot of money?
No, he didn't lose much.

Now continue in the same way.

Exercise 6

Listen to Jane talking to her friend in the office on Monday morning. She is telling her about her week in London. Then fill in the diary below with these places:

Gatwick Airport	Hotel	Oxford Street
Cinema	Zoo	British Museum
Serpentine	Market	Serpentine bar
Theatre	(Portobello Road)	Chinese restaurant
(The Mousetrap)	Discotheque	National Gallery

	Morning	Afternoon	Evening
Tuesday			
Wednesday			
Thursday			
Friday			
Saturday			
Sunday			

Unit Three Listening Exercises and Structure Drills

Exercise 1

Look at these examples and listen, please.

(read/a book)   What have you been doing?
                I've been reading a book.

(play/tennis)   What have they been doing?
                They've been playing tennis.

Now continue in the same way, using the information below.

1. do/her homework	4. study/English	7. lie/on the beach
2. drink/beer	5. write/a letter	8. have/lunch
3. practise/my English	6. sit/in a classroom	

Exercise 2

Look at these examples and listen, please.

(5 mins)   How long have you been waiting?
           For five minutes.

Now continue in the same way.

1. 2 yrs.	3. 6 mths.
2. 2½ hrs.	4. 10 wks.

Look at this example and listen again.

(yesterday)   How long have you been here?
              Since yesterday.

Now continue in the same way.

1. Christmas.	3. Mon.
2. last year.	4. 9.00.

Now answer these questions. Decide if you should use "for" or "since".

1. 3 days	5. his birthday
2. last month.	6. Sat. evening.
3. a quarter of an hour.	7. 11 mths.
4. 5 yrs.	8. Easter.

Exercise 3

Look at these examples and listen, please.

What are you doing?
I'm waiting for the rain to stop.
How long have you been waiting.

What is she doing?
She's sleeping.
How long has she been sleeping?

Now YOU ask the questions below. When you hear the answer ask how long its been happening, like in the examples.

1.* What are you doing?	4.* What is he doing?
2.* What is she doing?	5.* What are you doing?
3.* What are they doing?	6.* What are they doing?

Exercise 4

Listen please.

Was your lesson boring?
Yes, it was the most boring lesson I've ever had.

Is the wine sweet?
Yes, it's the sweetest wine I've ever had.

Now continue in the same way.

Exercise 5

Listen to the dialogue and then fill in the missing words below. Mrs Sampson is in bed with flu. Her husband has taken the day off work to look after her.

MR SAMPSON: How are you _____ now? Any _____ ?

MRS SAMPSON: What have _____ downstairs? I could hear the most terrible noise. Is _____ ?

MR SAMPSON: I've _____ the washing up.

MRS SAMPSON: Well, I hope you haven't _____ .

MR SAMPSON: Broken anything? Of course not. And _____ cooking too.

MRS SAMPSON: Cooking? But you don't even know how _____ an egg.

MR SAMPSON: I've made _____ nice bowl of soup.

MRS SAMPSON: That's not cooking. All you had to do was _____ .

	What _____ the sitting room? _____ hoovered it?
MR SAMPSON:	Yes, yes. I hoovered the sitting room _____ ago.
MRS SAMPSON:	Two days _____. Well it's not _____ then.
MR SAMPSON:	Well, it looks all right _____.
MRS SAMPSON:	Look. Don't let me shout __ you. I've _____ a terrible sore throat.
MR SAMPSON:	Then you _____ the soup I've made.
MRS SAMPSON:	Oh. And have you bought _____ cat food?
MR SAMPSON:	Yes, I have.
MRS SAMPSON:	And _____ for the weekend?
MR SAMPSON:	No, not ____. But _____ so much. Now would you ____ __ have the soup? It'll do you good.
MRS SAMPSON:	All right, dear. Thank you. You are ____ __ __ really? What's that funny smell?

Exercise 6

Listen to the passage and then fill in the table below. Use "more" + adjective or the "-er" form of the adjective in the correct way in the boxes to compare the two doctors. The first one has been done for you.

	Dr Walters	Dr Smythe
OLD		*older*
FAR		
SYMPATHETIC		
SHORT hours		
EASY to make an appointment		
MODERN surgery		
CROWDED waiting room		
NICE waiting room		
HANDSOME		

Unit Four Listening Exercises and Structure Drills

Exercise 1

Listen please.

Have you done your homework?
No, I'm sorry, I'm afraid I haven't.

Can you have dinner with me tonight?
No, I'm sorry, I'm afraid I can't.

Now continue in the same way.

Exercise 2

Listen please.

I haven't had a holiday for two years.
Neither have I.

I like to drive very fast.
So do I.

Now continue in the same way.

Exercise 3

Look at Jane's diary and listen, please.

What's Jane doing this Saturday evening?
She's going to the disco with Tom.

When is she meeting him?
She's meeting him at half past seven.

Now you answer the questions.

SAT 20	Disco with Tom meet 7.30
SUN 21	Cinema with Dick
MON 22	Stay home STUDY!!
TUES 23	Badminton with Harry
WED 24	Dinner Party make spaghetti
THURS 25	Yoga class 6.30 bed early
FRI 26	FLIGHT A 123 to Paris 8.45 pm
SAT 27	Day in Paris
SUN 28	FLIGHT A124 Arr Gatwick 11.10 am

Exercise 4

A mother is talking to her child. Look at these pictures and listen, please.

Picture 1
Why is he crying?
Because his mother told him to tidy his room.

Picture 2
Why is he crying?
Because his mother told him not to turn on the television.

Now you say why the child is crying.

Exercise 5

Read these sentences and try to put the stress in the right place. Then listen and repeat the sentences.

> 1.* A photographer takes photographs.
> 2.* A politician is interested in politics.
> 3.* An economist studies economics.
> 4.* An industrialist works in industry.
> 5.* An advertiser designs advertisements.
> 6.* A mathematician studies mathematics.

Exercise 6

Mr Markham is writing an article for a women's magazine about marriage. Listen to this interview he recorded with Mrs Gold and then answer the questions.

1. Why did Mrs Gold's first marriage end?

   _____

2. Why did her second marriage end?

   _____

3. Is her third husband alive or dead?

Put a tick in the correct box on the right.

4. Mrs Gold's first husband was a) lazy
                                 b) sociable
                                 c) handsome

5. Mrs Gold's second husband was a) attractive
                                  b) amusing
                                  c) faithful

6. Mrs Gold's third husband is a) untidy
                                b) good with his hands
                                c) hard-working

True	False	Don't know